Midnight Sun / Catherine Czerkawska

**ALSO BY CATHERINE CZERKAWSKA**

**Fiction**

The Curiosity Cabinet
The Posy Ring
The Jewel
The Physic Garden
Bird of Passage
The Amber Heart
Ice Dancing
Rewilding
A Bad Year for Trees and other stories

**Non Fiction**

The Way It Was
For Jean: Poems, Songs and Letters by Robert Burns
for his wife Jean Armour
Precious Vintage
A Proper Person to be Detained
The Last Lancer

**Plays**

Wormwood
The Price of a Fish Supper
Quartz
Burns on the Solway
The Secret Commonwealth

# *Midnight Sun*

COLLECTED POEMS BY

Catherine Czerkawska

Published by Dyrock Publishing



Cover image by Michał Piasecki

ISBN: 978-1-7384205-0-6

# CONTENTS

## LATER POEMS: A MISCELLANY

## INTRODUCTION

People often ask me when I first started writing, but the truth is that I can't remember a precise time. I had serious asthma as a child, and, with treatments less than effective back then, I spent a lot of time away from school. It suited me. We were a working class Leeds Irish household, albeit one with an 'alien' addition, in the shape of my wonderful Polish refugee dad. It was a household that loved books. We had a stack of old Wonder Books that had belonged to one of my older aunts: big anthologies of extracts from the classics, folk tales, fairy tales and poems. These were illustrated by artists like Arthur Rackham, Anne Anderson, Jessie M King and a host of others, and they were inspirational. Nobody lectured me on what I ought to read. Nobody ever sourced worthy educational books as a way of teaching me to behave. But I read constantly and widely, so writing just seemed like a natural progression.

I know that I began with poetry.

When I was twelve, we moved to Ayrshire in Scotland. Woefully unhappy – an 'interlowper' to use the Scots word – at school, I took refuge in books and history and the work of our local poet, Robert Burns. At weekends, I walked out to Burns Cottage, daydreaming. During my teens, poetry was still my main interest, although because I had listened to so much radio drama throughout those early years of illness, I was trying my hand at that as well.

At the age of seventeen, I went off to Edinburgh University to study English Language and Literature, specialising in Mediaeval Studies, a much happier time of my life, one where I made lifelong friends. I spent some of my spare time there working on poems and occasional short stories, publishing them, reviewing books, doing readings here, there and everywhere and, once I had graduated, embarking on the drama writing that would see me produce more than a hundred hours of radio drama over the next twenty years or so. All the same, I carried on writing poems, and I published a couple of pamphlets, as well as numerous contributions to literary magazines, some of which are listed at the back of this compilation.

When I was hunting through my old magazines, anthologies, broadsheets and pamphlets, in the process of editing this collection, it struck me how fortunate we were as young writers, back in the 70s and 80s, with the number of outlets to which we could submit our work. Magazines such as Scottish International, edited by Bob Tait, published new poetry alongside political and arts analyses and reviews. BBC Radio Scotland was still broadcasting poetry by relative unknowns. Edinburgh University played host to three poetry festivals (Poem 72, 73 and 74) brilliantly organised by postgraduate student John Schofield, with help from beginners like myself. When I remember that time, I'm blown away, not just by the 'big names' of poetry who were willing to come along and read, but by the sheer enthusiasm for the work.

At the same time, it was the beginning of the end of an era when poetry in Scotland had largely been a male preserve, as had so much else. When I graduated in 1972, there was a whole slew of jobs I couldn't apply for. I wouldn't even have been able to apply for a mortgage in my own name. Alexander Moffat's celebrated painting of the Poet's Pub, in Rose Street, depicted male poets, with the women relegated to the traditional but unenviable position of the literary muse. You have only to look at the editorial names at the end of this collection to see how few women were part of the literary establishment. Still, times seemed to be changing, although not all that much, as I would later discover after one or two less-than-happy early experiences with Scottish theatre. But we were reading Germaine Greer and Simone de Beauvoir, and we refused to be excluded.

Suddenly, there were well attended poetry readings here, there and everywhere. There were good, accessible performance spaces such as the Third Eye Centre in Glasgow and the old Traverse in Edinburgh and, more vitally, there were audiences. Practising poets and novelists (without the now obligatory creative writing degrees) were writers in residence in academic institutions. The old Scottish Arts Council distributed small amounts of funding, with advice and encouragement from real practitioners, male and female.

Some time in the mid 1980s, while I was happily married, bringing up a child, working on plays for radio and theatre, and publishing fiction, I felt that my own poetry slowly but surely dried up. Perhaps there was no more room for it. It seemed to me that when I wrote fiction, I was exercising the same 'muscle' that had once produced poetry. I wondered if it would ever come back. More recently, as I worked on a couple of demanding and very personal pieces of non-fiction (*A Proper Person to be Detained* and *The Last Lancer*) I somehow found poetry tugging at my imagination again. Whether I'll ever really go back to it or not remains to be seen. I'm certainly going back to fiction with a certain amount of relief, and there's a sense in which the poetry informs the fiction. It strikes me now that I've always written my fiction and even non-fiction in the same way as I wrote these poems, working from instinct, with very little planning, but then polishing constantly through many drafts. Writing to find out.

All this prompted me to dig out the paper folders and computer files containing what amounted to half a lifetime of poetry. To my surprise, many of them were not half bad. Some of them were old love poems, but none the worse for that. Some reflected the (literal) journeys I had made as a young woman. Most of them had been published in one way or another, a few had even won prizes, so other people had found them 'not half bad' back then. Most still have the power to move me, to remind me of past times, past dilemmas, past joys and sorrows.

Here they are, a selection, roughly chronologically arranged. There's a part of me that has gathered all these poems together just for myself. They remind me of all the work and care that went into them, over so many years. If they strike a chord with readers, that will be a bonus.

I hope you enjoy them.

*Catherine Czerkawska, Ayrshire, 2024*

## EARLY POEMS

Some of my earliest poems should, of course, never see the light of day again. You have to serve an apprenticeship. The best piece of advice I ever had (from, as far as I remember, the late Angus Wolfe Murray) was, 'Stop watering your Dylan Thomas adjectives and watching them grow.' How right he was. This is a selection of my older poems of which I'm not ashamed, many of which managed to find a publisher at the time.

## CUT GLASS

Oh speak to me of things that do not matter.
Our friendship is a fragile thing.
Speak too loudly and
it will shatter.

Each self is patterned with
the other self.
We are similar but not the same,
surrounded with a tissue
of touches now and then
or compliments.
The light shines through us,
is distorted.
We both pretend
not to know
that this fragile thing
if subject to one outright blow
would shatter.

Take care.
Oh speak to me of things that do not matter.

## FOR ANNOT AND JOHN

In the years 1250 to 1300
the summers were finer than before or since.
Some poet before me wrote of
gyngyure and sedewale and the gylofre
by which he meant that these were
his little Anne. Ginger, valerian and the
gillyflower were precious.
Some living, breathing, walking man
whose name was John has left us
a pot pourri of words
for the sunlight to shine upon. It dried
and dried the fallen petals around his pen.
Her name was in a note of the nightingale.
In his garden when he wrote of singing birds
it is possible to smell the garden in his words.

## THREAD

If I love you
your life instantly becomes
more fragile than my own,
your body more frail,
each cough or minor pain
a symptom of some dread
disease or other.

Death is on every road
or in every other car.
Some nights my skin
flutters in apprehension
and I am so threatened that
caring translates itself
inside my head to
stone cold anger

because I am insufficient,
tormented by the frailty
of you whom I love.
Selfish I
find you
necessary for my definition.
Your life is a single thread.
It snaps.
I wither.

## ALIENS

I am small in springtime
on my father's shoulders.
I can see everything even the
bald patches on the
heads of passing men,
a precarious and thrilling position.

My father's hair is coal black and curly,
Polish hair as foreign as he is.
The word refugee is as familiar
to me as my own name.
I hold his ears for balance,
while he trots with me aloft.

My father's papers proclaim him alien
which makes me half alien too.
Poland might as well be Pluto but
the iron curtain is real.
I see it sweeping across Europe
made of polished metal,
dividing kin from kin,
as unfathomable as space.

Small and safe on his shoulders,
his hands steadying me,
I grip his ears and laugh.
We are what we will always be
to one another: complicit and loving
alien invaders of
a mystifying new world.

## LOVE AND GUILT

My grandfather went fishing in summer.
He came back with bunches of flowers and
baskets of cherries but with very few fish.

I sat with him in his dusty shop
where a pike skulked in a glass case.
He sold maggots in jam jars
to anglers in cloth caps.
They wore watch chains and had
Yorkshire woollen waistcoats
stretched across their bellies.
They called him by his first name.
Ey up Joe, they said.

The maggots lived in a tin bath.
He flavoured them with curry powder
for enigmatic reasons of his own.
Once they escaped and the
house was full of bluebottles for days.

My grandfather was a big man with
grey hair that looked as though it had been
stitched in ridges on his neck.
He had sailed to Singapore on
the last of the tea clippers.
A blue snake wound around his arm.
I would trace it with my fingers, the
way his muscles moved beneath the skin
bringing the serpent to life.

My grandfather was a Methodist but
I made him learn the Catholic catechism
Who made you God made me.
Meekly he would recite the words,
a lamb to my imperious demands.

He had a passion for Tizer.
It made me sick but I wheedled.
We drank it together and
when I was very sick
I blamed him.

In future I would betray myself to
lost lovers with retributions
more shameful than sickness
forgetting that such adoration is rare.
Much too easy to learn those first
paradigms of love, blackmail, guilt.

His eyes grew milky.
Oh my little queen he would say,
running his sailor's hands over my
head to feel the silky pigtails tied with red.

## OVEN BOTTOM CAKES

My Irish nana made oven bottom cakes
with the last of the dough,
furiously working the elastic on
cold marble, her hair thrust back
like a schoolgirl's with a clip.
I see her print pinafore and her body
flex as she presses her thumb into
the middle of each cake then
leans across the rag rug to throw
deft flour into the oven to judge
if the temperature is right.

On a February morning in smoky Leeds
in 1910, my nana, a shirt maker,
gave birth to twin girls, Gladys and Ethel.
She named no father and they died within months
of malnutrition and convulsions.
Later, she told nobody.
They were erased from our story
as surely as if they had never lived
until years after her death when
some remote cousin gleefully
excavating the family tree,
sniffed them out and spilt the beans.

Toddling, I would nap with her
in the afternoons and she would
push me out of her bed for
fidgeting, my soft breasted nan.
Did she see in me those
babies she had buried?
My nana baked bread for me.
How she loved to feed me good things,
made oven bottom cakes and we'd
eat them with the best butter
and blackberry jam that
nipped your teeth with seeds.

## SMOG

My dad was late.
Outside the smog settled on the city.
The meal dried up and filled the room
with the stench of burnt vegetables.
Mum fussed, riled by her unease.
I lay on the couch, wheezing.
The inability to breathe dogged my nights,
worse when these beasts
all yellow tongues and tails
crept beneath the door and curled around the lights.

When dad came home, dazed and pale,
he wore a bandage over one eye.
A car had collided with his bike.
Next day a strong wind blew the smog away
but I lay dazed by the realisation that
anything could happen.
My worst fears might come true.
People were fragile, all brittle bones and blood.
It could happen over and over again
and probably would.

## POEM FOR MY FATHER

If you regret
that I do not seem
proud enough of you
for small achievements,
do not forget
that I save
the greatest for the great
which is
for all you have lost and fought
you do not hate.
And I have never heard
one phrase of bitterness
over the war which
tore your life apart.
Like those who pieced
Warsaw together,
stone by stone,
when you rebuilt
you did so from the heart.

As I perhaps could not
you have stood the test.
My words are poor as
they are magnificent.
Of all great men
you are the best.

## SUDDEN MAN *(for the late Tony Green)*

He's a sudden man
and alarming. He
fills rooms like plastic foam,
flings brown paper sounds
around you like synthetic thunder.
He's as eloquent as hell.
He'll throw half a brick of
critical interrogation at you
to get your measure and
maybe lay you out as well.
He's prickly. Got an edge
but all that's sham
because you find
where words are easier
and less precise,
he's suddenly kind.

And it's this sudden warmth
that really disturbs you
some spark that will
kindle and ignite
into a conflagration,
expand and crackle into
astonishing speculation.

Such frail flames
that suddenly die.
How abruptly a little water
will extinguish him.

## THE FOX

### 1

The fox walked through an autumn dark,
his skin alert, his nose involved
in a hundred scents
all shifting towards decay.
His flesh cried for flesh.
In a little pool
fringed with mist,
flat and thick dark, he
saw a perfect moon reflected.

Her beauty quickened his heart,
plump as a cherry to bite and suck.
His head full of the moon,
the fox's eyes flew right and left.
Now he would have her
deftly and like a scragged chicken
by the neck.
Chicken or cherry was all one
to itching teeth.

The fox pounced.

But the deceitful moon sailed on
and the lunatic fox dripped home,
hungry.

2

The fox is a red flame.
He sees his black shadow on a stone,
sidling along the edges of hills,
feels his muscles flex,
bites and is not bitten.

The fox does not know his own name
but grins when the sunlight strikes
the tip of his tail and tells him
killing time.

## 3

She met him out in the sun,
eyes sharp, teeth ready for her,
knew him, too frightened
to turn away.
His blood was up and
crying for her in
short, imperious barks.
He judged her weaknesses
came slowly close.
She saw how the red hairs on him were
turning grey
but fox she knew him when
he licked his lips and bit off
the first kiss.

## BOSS

Like a wee fat cock he
struts among hens all
pride and show.
A peck or swift pat on
one cheek or another
here and there.
His ladies smile and flutter and
make tea. Where would he be without
his ladies?
Ratatat go their sharp heels
down his whip and leather dreams.
He smiles a wee fat smile,
so swollen feather full
he will presently
throw back his head and
crow and crow and crow.

## KEYSTONE COP *(for Harry, 1971)*

I knew a policeman once
though out of uniform and
out of role he was still
my polisman my fuzzy wuzzy
my piglet my bobby my
own fair cop.
That's how it was therefore
I'm prejudiced anti-establishment
(the many) and
pro polis
(just the one).

It was the fuzz after all who
placated the fisherman
in the Chinese Restaurant
shouting it was shrimp
not prawn curry;
he should know he said
as he spat out mouthfuls of
chewed pink proof.

It was the fuzz who
waltzed around a lamp-post
in the street late for loneliness
pretending it was Raquel Welsh,
who whistled at girls from his box
and pretended he didn't,
who tripped over a drunk in the dark
and pretended he hadn't.

It was the fuzz who
collected a lost dog and
took it home, who
propped up the old man
and held him with gentle hands
as his tears fell down
plop onto the pavement,
who came after the Sudden Death
and was kind.

That's how it was
so none of your proletarian games.
Don't try to kick his teeth in.
Don't call him nasty names,
my fuzzy wuzzy my polisman
my law and order custodian
my piglet my bobby my bluebottle
my own fair cop.

## AT THE TOP OF THE WOODS

We lie together at the very top of the woods.
Are these dragons, drowning the sun in smoke,
clawing through dead wood,
where small animals are afraid and burrow?

Or perhaps he is the sleek unicorn
with a gleaming body
who knows not half his strength
and is unaware of me thinking

that I too am a small animal and afraid,
burrowing into my own head,
fearing the discord of dragons
in treasured splendour through these summer woods.

He knows only some harmony of my body and his,
knows the large domestic dog
snuffling at our feet and the crows in our sky
and no mystery of himself, dragons or unicorns either.

## GLASGOW QUARTET

### SNAPSHOT

A photograph is all I have
representing a thin, bright
sliver of my time.
Even then I thought of needing it.
Your newspaper sheltered you.
It is still in the picture.
The Times, it was,
simply a matter of, you knew.
You were already moving on.
I used to read the Guardian myself,
preferring to save moments,
not squander them. If I could
I would go backwards
gathering fragments among
the ages that made me. So
the gap was widening between us.
I quickly caught your
big smile in the sun.
Here it is, between the pages of a book,
the slight part of you
that I knew.
Only a thin, bright sliver of my time.

## CATHEDRAL

One late summer day
spent with you in a
touch too much of the sun.
Hot city and uncompromisingly
Glasgow. Warts and all.

Another grim cathedral.
Ghosts in a cold cold crypt.
Shadows where I left you cold.
Cold insinuating to the bone.
Nothing was sacred really.

Outside the Necropolis
clung crawling to the hill,
urns and John Knox,
thoughts of an ostentatious death.
I was terrified.

Oh I loved you in spite of
my tired feet in tight shoes.
Love made me numb. But
we were a poor match.
You found me ill fitting.

## HILLHEAD

November. How it rained.
How it rained when
fat and sad in black
I ran to your house,
rang the bell and
made a pretence of anger,
running up the stairs
to a room where
your small hands shaped
graceful words around you.

You had grown thin and brittle
like a bird.
I could see your wings upon the wall.
My words flew out like feathers
to fleece them.
You meant to fly and
you were not afraid to fall.

Again outside
against the soft hiss
of rainy traffic,
our quick breath smoked,
we passed by tattered leaves,
dead rainbows in gutters,
we shared a last umbrella and
a cold, cold kiss.

## NOW

Sometimes now
on my way to visit
other friends
who live in the same place,
I think that there
you live too.
And I cannot now
even ring the bell
and climb the stair
to drink tea or pass
the time of day with you.

I wrecked our friendship
on love's precipitous reef.

Sometimes now
I lie awake and think
with a kind of shock
how I saw you
in Hillhead Station
and ran away,
up into the busy street.
Dear God. Even the
instinctive dogs stop
and sniff each other
when they meet.

## POEMS FROM FINLAND

For two very happy years, back in the mid 1970s, I taught English conversation to adults, mostly business people, in a private language school in Tampere. It was hard work, but – not being in possession of a television, and with the World Wide Web hardly even a gleam in 20 year old Tim Berners-Lee's eye - I could do plenty of exciting things, mostly courtesy of my students. I went to ice hockey games, learned (after a fashion) how to do cross country ski-ing, was invited for weekends in summer cottages with wonderful saunas, went for long walks across frozen lakes, flew over the town in a Cessna with one of the subjects of these poems, and was occasionally invited out for meals by nice young engineers who earned more than I could dream of. I also managed to write a novel that still sits in a bottom drawer, and a heap of poems about the experience, including the title poem of this collection.

Here are some of them.

## THE LAND OF WOOD

I sailed to the land of wood,
thrusting the sea aside to find
the ragged tops of pines
cutting the sky like paper.

People were trees.
Spruce and larch and linden
walked the streets while
here and there a long
willow boy swayed with
fragile drunken grace.

In spring the first new
scent was trees
and the first tree was
*koivu*, bright birch,
his leaves tossing
coins of light.
I saw him once
casting back his head
in the sunshine and
could not forget it.

I wanted to be a small spider
nestling in his hollow shoulder
where it was warm. Then
while he was sleeping,
with a sweet and steady breath,
I would come quietly
and look at him.

But never again
from the deep shadowed eye
to the lips will I
dare to spin a tender web of
love into words for him.

For who knows the
seasons of a tree?
Autumn must be deadly.
Who knows how the ebbing strength
aches in them, nor what
evil of ice enters in?

Who knows the mind
when the heart is carved of wood?

## MIDNIGHT SUN

Is it day or night?
The city streets
clasp the heat fast and
late drunks tumble home to sleep.

Is it day or night?
In the warm forest
marsh marigolds jostle for a place,
small lilies crouch in hooded green,
confused thrushes chatter
like shattered glass.

Is it day or night?
Small creatures furrow
lightly on the lake in
random, purposeful lines.
Mosquitos pilot in and bite.
Black beetles toddle to the
water's edge.
The surface is streaked with
pollen, soft as a man's hair.

Is it night or day?
The sun that makes a narrow angle
with the lake's thin line
considers for a moment
along the slender
very rim of the dark
and rises again.

## CLOUDBERRIES

Cloudberries are rare these days.
You can search all day
among the marshes. Meanwhile
mosquitoes feed on you.

When you bring them in a pail,
though you have picked for hours,
fingers torn, face swollen, they will
subside slowly to fewer than
you would ever have believed.

Dreamberries dissolving between the teeth
with a faint golden taste of the sky.

## LOOK

Look how the shiny
night time square
gleams with water.
Nothing is still,
not the light in puddles,
not the sleepless tossing wind.

Nothing is ever still.

## DUCKS

Lord love the ducks in
Tammerkoski pool,
sleek ducks
the town feeds, gratis.
They have no god
only this congenial paper mill
to warm their baths.

They do not care for paper
nor see us struggling to work,
stifling yawns, slipping
arse over tip in the snow
but huddle moodily
and dream of sauna or
griddles.
I suppose some even die.
Sorsat* requiescant.

* *Sorsat: ducks.*

## ACHIEVEMENTS

The ice has achieved itself again,
thick stalactites,
on roofs on cars on traffic lights.

Everything is static.
The cold chokes.
Even hand in hand shocks.

Each night the fine white
crystals drift into every crevice.
Soon we will give up trying to
sweep away the snow.

## AT THE PULP MILL

Afternoon, the December day already
bound for darkness.
The sky balloons over, rubbery
and forced to diffuse a taut glow.

Below, precarious structures
thrum and throb.
Lumbering bulldozers
totter along the pile of pulp,
drunken with the yellow
scent of pine and
pale crows flap
from tree to tree
remembering where
wheatfields once lay
fallow, winter long.

Here it is all hemming
binding and building,
a crazed struggle to contain,
but the banished wind's
crafty breath finds gaps
in the construction and
elsewhere the innocent ice
locks the lake logs with a
more ruthless efficiency.

Still man muddles on,
his meddlesome fingers
and all his sad alchemy
conjuring a mad beauty
from the stubborn land.

## DRUNKS IN WINTER

The big drunks are
waltzing homewards through the snow,
their cloudy heads fur hatted,
their feet thrust deep
into clumsy boots.
They fear no cold.
Instead they spread
their arms wide for love
and when they go,
they topple like felled trees,
with a dull thud.

## ROOF TROLLS

Two roof trolls
dressed in red and blue
heft blocks of solid snow
off tops.

One squats behind a chimney
doffs his hat and
lights his pipe. Grinning,
the other plants his troll's feet
fair and right to prize up
ice with a shining shovel.

Whoosh and thud.
Oh watch your heads below.
The roof trolls are above.

## WINTER

Cold and heavy
like a world ending
the sky over that white field.

Field or lake?
Crow tracks along the fringes,
the trees are mere sticks, thin
bronchitics, rubbing each other up
the wrong way.

At minus twenty five
the hairs inside your
nostrils are tinged with frost and
clean through three wool mittens
old Jack pinches.

## JORMA (1)

A stocky puppy
waits for me each week
with old gold fur.
He's lazy, truculent and
charming by turns and
like a puppy would
bully if he dared.

He's sweet and twenty.
I paint my nails bright
brown for him, wear scent,
feel more than my
three years older.
But how we laugh,
daft laughter without
wit or edge.

Come closer for I am
blinded by the sight of your
eyes, how curious like
big blue fishes
in your face. Warm eyes
they're sly and shy and
asking to be kissed but

when he rubs them I see
how grubby and
desperate and dangerous
is his small, clenched fist.

## JORMA (2)

In my mind, you are
a sudden geometry of logs
on the lake at Lielahti
or the brown rain of
linden leaves in Hameenkatu.

You are a man in sunshine boots
delicately sweeping the street,
a creamy curl of smoke
searching the frozen sky,
a buttercup yellow house
drenched in snow.
Your face lights rooms.

Even your hands on a cigarette
pierce me with their
small splendour.

But oh how your Midas touch
leaves me golden
and my heavy tongue
so sadly dumb to tell you.

## MY MAGPIES

Still one metre of spring snow with
the light growing.
I saw everything
in black and white.

My magpies. Men like paper
planes drifting across the sky.
You would have thought
two of them might have managed
some joy. But no.
I had to leave them.
They left me no alternative,
gave little, took all,
even the tears from my eyes because
they glistened.

## THAW

Autumn began it,
a cold breath
that sent colour
splashing down
among the leaves.

Soon everything was
snowed under.
You crystallised my heart.
No frosts could wither me.
We entered into
the kingdom of the snow.

But it is springtime that kills.
I have cried out all my thawed heart
and still the warm drowned space
aches for you.

## PINEAPPLES

A short policeman
whistles us across the street.
How stout and sweet how
gaily spins his baton,
how deft, admire me,
he thinks and we agree.

There is a troll ahead,
a troll in the street.
What buses do trolls take?
He is holding a season ticket,
a law abiding troll.
There are hordes of trolls
with flat faces and gorgeous
old gold hair but
a little stony,
beware, beware.

The trees are full of birds and
last year's apples
under a cold blue sun.
The shop is unexpectedly
full of pineapples.

My lover has left me.
Sing hey he was a stony troll too.
I shall be warm and
wicked and eat
one whole pineapple
for the hell of it.

## AHMA*

Ahma is black and shaggy,
smaller than a bear,
climbs trees and
lurks there.

When the foolish
reindeer walks below,
Ahma drops and
hangs on sucking
sweet blood
until men
come with weapons
and spill his own.

Each does as he must.
But here and there
you see his shadow,
the form of a black
beast without compassion,
lolloping by.

* *wolverine*

## MATTI'S DAUGHTER (1)

Matti's daughter is so new
she glistens like
the small, tough grass after rain.

She has four years to count,
not even one whole handful.
Still, she balances them
with grave deliberation.

## MATTI'S DAUGHTER (2)

Tiny, she clutches at my hand
all smiles and
Look, she says, I'll draw you
a giraffe.
One long, bold line is
hurled across the page
with a peal of laughter.
Look, she says, grasping concepts
in two small fists and
hugging them tight.
A giraffe.

## HILLE

Long legged Hille
knocking at my door
cheers me.

Quick fingered,
bright witted
girl, sunny as
marigolds

Golden girl with a
deer's sleek grace,
dear doe
bright dear
puts sunshine smiling
on winter's face.

## APRIL

Long days of April, deliquescent days.
Things shifted.
Gladly we flew over the melting city to
see factory and forest
creep clear of winter.
A curlew like a new bird
crazed the airfield
and it rained
for the first time that year.

Below was different.
Walking was suddenly easy.
There was joy in running.
Shunning small safe steps
we hurried like other folk,
beat mats,
cleaned windows,
changed tyres.

But the blue bloom of snow
had gone, leaving
a haggard town
and who was now secure,
locked tight in
winter's kind abeyance?

That night, a big wind
shattered the packed lake ice.
Infirmity yawned.
We clung to streets where
last year's litter lay
in sodden heaps.

We knew we knew why
in bleak rooms between seasons
suicides retched and slept.
Oh this year
we came through,
buried our naked days
beneath May's swift green,
dressed ourselves lightly
and set our winter clothes to rest.

But next year, another April,
will we be men and women
made of snow?
For when the sunlight
shines on them
they cringe, they dwindle
and they go.

## POEMS FROM POLAND

After my time in Finland, I spent a year in Poland, teaching English conversation to senior students at Wroclaw University. This was more challenging, not because of the students, who were consistently loveable, but because this was Poland, still under Soviet sway. I had to surrender my passport on arrival. The post was sponsored by the British Council, which gave me a certain amount of security. It wasn't my first time in Poland. I had visited much loved relatives there before, and there were ways in which it felt like home. But when you saw a queue outside a shop, you always joined it first and asked what you were queuing for later. And you had to be careful not to make political statements during classes. I was lucky to have an apartment to myself, albeit one with a phone that was tapped, and hard currency to spend in the shops where only foreigners and party members could go - some animals being more equal than others. Most of my writing from that year involved a tapestry of short stories, plays and a few articles. Nevertheless, from time to time, I found myself working on poems, because nothing else would do.

## POTATO FIRES

I remember
talking with my uncle Karol,
walking arm in arm
on Polish evenings when
mist spread over flat fields
and women were burning
the last of the potato leaves.

We wrinkled our nostrils.
It was a kind of myrrh for us,
preserving the moment yet
bitterly telling time.

There was no cure for it.
Though I hurtled through youth
for love of him
he's gone too far before.

## ANDRZEJ

War pared down his heart.
He lost too much
ever to be safe again.
Now he lives every day
as if it were his last,
as hard and warm as
the dogs, the horses
that love him.

In the Warsaw cemetery
his eyes grow black with rage.
There is evidence of battle:
frayed stones, bullet holes.
Acres of anonymous dead
lie among the trees
with a few candles sprouting
like flowers between them.
He falls silent, then,
in our mutual French, tells me,
*Mon père, il est mort, a Katyn.*
*Il n'avait pas des chandelles.*

I still see him, Andrzej,
in his forest house,
kindling fires for guests,
anxious to please,
raging that he was born too late.

But how else could such
hospitality light on us?
Look, there are squirrels at his window
and even the old wild wood
comes creeping to his gate.

## UNCLE KAROL AT CIECHOCINEK

The day we went to the cemetery
I was so choked with asthma
I thought I might die.
Snow clouds scurried by.
The wind seized me.
The wind wrenched my breath.
The wind squeezed me,
squeezed the weak tears
from my eyes.

We lit some candles for him
but I could not imagine
him down there or anywhere,
the long, brave, elegant
length of him,
no breath,
however hard I tried.

## DOG IN WROCŁAW

A dog, smooth little
mongrel, snub nosed and
barrel chested, trots out of the
doorway on four short legs
into the sun

sniffs the Indian summer air
haunted by drains and sauerkraut,
sweat, diesel, cigarettes but
over there a great
green scent assaults his nose.

Twice he tries to cross the busy road:
a motor cycle swings round fast and
back he goes, cringing, then a
lorry, monstrous, roaring down, he
swerves and shoots out undeterred,
black bullet head fixed firm

straight for the golden park where he will
dance all bravado now and
cock his stiff white legs on trees
ah countless trees and
sniff the changed air
like a dog.

## LEECH SONG

May brings lovers to the street,
heads touching, limbs slant with desire.
I know my love by his way of walking.

The market folk have flooded out like sunshine.
On the pavement are
apples, aprons, laces.

The leech woman crouches
calling *pi-jav-ki,*
three solemn syllables.
They creep obscenely round
glass prisons, *pi-jav-ki.*
Who buys them?
They are said to thin the blood
makes the blood
and if my love leave me
run cold.

Bonny boys are few.
If I could buy poems
like hyacinths
dressed in a suit of blue
I would send them to you.
But I will carve them instead
from the white page.

Walk with me my beloved
come summer,
limbs slant with desire,
heads touching.

## GNATS

Somewhere in the wild east
great grandfather drank
thirty cups of tea a day
from a silver samovar.
Great granny was a countess.
Doubtless she spoke French.
The parties were magnificent.
There were nightingales in the gardens
but also gnats.
While nightingales poured
molten notes through the trees -
lindens they were and
full of flowers and bees -
the gnats came inside.
Gnats need a listener.
At night the gnats sang
a thin little song,
a sad gnat song,
so that the high humming
flowed on through each
sleeper's dream.
One never saw a gnat.
One only heard.
They were invisible,
profoundly disturbing,
sadder than nightingales,
tenuous as freedom,
just a thin little song
in the dark.

## LATER POEMS: A MISCELLANY

Returning from Poland, I worked as Community Writer for the Arts in Fife for a couple of years, before eventually coming back to Ayrshire in 1980, and marrying my lovely husband, Alan Lees, who was a professional charter yacht skipper. After the birth of our son, he came ashore to build and restore rocking horses, undertake massive outdoor woodcarvings, and – more recently – turn his hand to painting. I wrote full time. And here we are, all these years later, still writing and painting.

I wrote poems from time to time, and when I look back, there are more of them than I thought. Often, as with the Robert Burns related poems, they seemed to be written in conjunction with other projects that were obsessing me at the time, such as my novel, The Jewel, about the poet's largely unsung wife, Jean Armour. Sometimes family sorrows drew me back to poetry. I was writing plays for the Traverse and the Oran Mor as well as for BBC R4, working on nine published novels (and a few more that languish in that bottom drawer along with the Finnish novel) short stories and several big historical non-fiction projects. I also worked for the Royal Literary Fund as a Writing Fellow for an enjoyable four years, helping students with their academic writing.

## BURNS ON THE SOLWAY (1)

Here at the Brow Well on the Solway
I come to the edge of the land and almost
tumble into a mass of thrift, clumps of pink
fringing the shore like some wild garden.

I go struggling and staggering into the sea,
half a mile each day, far enough for the water to
reach to my waist as the doctors say I must.
The seawater does some good
only in that it numbs the pain.
The wind blows unhindered across the mud.
The sky is dazzling with the glitter of a
sun half hidden behind clouds
as I walk out again and again.

Sometimes I feel flounders
slithering away beneath my feet.
My landlady tells me that she would go
flounder trampling when she was a lassie,
kilting up her skirts and wading out into the Firth,
feeling for fishes with her toes.

She fills my bottle with port wine.
I can swallow little else.
I say that the muckle black deil
has got into my wallet.
I offer her my seal in payment
but she shakes her head.
Put it away Mr Burns, she says.

June with its briars and its sweet
burnet roses was my last summer.
Here at the Brow Well on the Solway,
I come to the edge of the land and almost
fall into a mass of thrift, clumps of brown
rustling along the shore like some dying garden.

## BURNS ON THE SOLWAY (2)

July and the year has turned.
If I could regain my strength
I would make shift to sift my work.
I have not put my papers in any
state of arrangement.
There are many indifferent pieces which
I fear will be thrust upon the world
with all their imperfections on their head.
There are ballads bearing my name
being hawked about the streets of Dumfries.
What in the name of God will they
do with me when I am dead?

There is a farmer at Locharwoods
with a gig and what my landlady
pleases to call a gentry horse.
She tells me he will be glad to lend me both
so that I can win back to Jean,
but I have no inclination save to
stretch out in the small shade of this
hawthorn and watch the birds
fly over the Solway.

Who knows where sky ends,
where water gives place to sand?
The laverocks climb to the very edge of sound
like my words in my wife's mouth,
like my lips on hers,
like my songs on her lips,
and at my naked feet
the silvery meander of a burn
finally meeting the sea.

## CLARINDA*

It was not charm. I know about charm.
James McLehose was charming
bought all the seats on the coach
from Glasgow so that he could
have me to himself without interruption.
He gave me food and wine at the inn,
spoke gently and smiled.
Twelve hours later I fancied myself in love.

After the wedding I knew my mistake.
Whisky was his mistress.
He loved her more than me
even when she incensed him.
When he took himself off to the Indies,
God forgive me I thought of what
foreign fevers could do to a man
and I prayed how I prayed
but the devil looks out for his own.

They said the poet had charm but
I know charm and it is not this.
I think he simply liked the company of women.
He was bedding my servant while he was
writing to me of love, but even now
my flesh remembers his fond kiss.
I joined James, leaving my bairns
with his kindly cousin Elizabeth

who in her notes to me misspelt even
her own name, Elizebath she wrote.
The air over the water was too hot to breathe and
smelled of outlandish flowers and swamps and sin.
James had a woman in his bed.
I glimpsed her luxurious hair, her long brown limbs.
I cannot say I blamed him.

I came home to find that Robert had married his Jean.
I grow old and paint my cheeks and regale my
Edinburgh patrons with tales of Clarinda and Sylvander.
What I remember best I keep to myself
the touch of his hands here and his lips here.
It was not charm nor was it love
but it is something to have been called
best and dearest by such a man.

* *Clarinda was Nancy McLehose, with whom Burns had an intense flirtation in Edinburgh. There was indeed a 'kindly cousin Elizabeth' who could not spell her own name. I have her pretty little Old Testament, in which she has written the details of her family, calling herself Elizebath. The poet wrote the achingly beautiful Ae Fond Kiss for Nancy. But he wrote Red Red Rose for Jean Armour and he married her.*

## THE DRIZZLER*

The play's the place for this game,
crowded halls, assemblies, balls.
I keep a pair of scissors in my
needle case, birds of steel, their
beaks as sharp as my tongue, and
a spool for winding my booty on.
My skirts are a garden,
how my nimble needle flies.
A froth of smuggled lace at my wrist
hides my hand from prying eyes.

Peacocks are my prey.
Rich young men or old no matter
so long as their coats are fancy.
Roses, purls and picots are good,
dangling spangles are easy,
acorns are fine, fringes are better
but I have grown so bold that
I have slit silver buttons from their
waistcoats beneath their noses
and I remember one young buck who
wore medallions of beaten gold
with cupids and I had them I had them but
I was sorry to send such cherubs for melting.

Some women call their pillage flirtation.
What can their gallants do but submit?
But the covert assault excites me more.
I gauge them from behind my fan.
Up close, their hearts beat far too loud to
hear the slice of blade on blade.
They never see my work.
They're watching the shady cleft
between my breasts, they never catch
the swiftness of my hand
between their baubles, but
with their warm lips on mine
I'll palm my shears and
clip their treasures one by one.

My mother died when I was
much too young to grieve.
My father pays lip service to thrift while
donning his powdered wigs, his velvets,
his hose, his ruffled linen shirts.
So I'll take what's offered elsewhere
snipping in secret, concealing my
rich pickings in my sleeve.

Later, I'll tease my stolen gold from
silken thread and take it to the old wife
who weighs it on her scales and
hands me a few coins instead.
Pin money. It's never enough,
but the thought of this subtle robbery
makes me flush and catch my breath.
I'll prick their vanity with my tiny shears.
A small piracy.
We are drizzlers.
We are buccaneers.

* *Drizzling was the largely female, eighteenth century practice of snipping precious metal embellishments from male garments, with or without the wearer's permission, and selling the gold and silver to be melted down.*

## GRAINNE*

Diarmuid paid me scant attention,
torn between honour and desire.
The old earl brought eggs and fish and
small dark fruits from the moors. He made me
a bed of curlew feathers, softer than heather.
I slept well there but I slept alone.

At last he came to me with a plan.
We would kill Diarmuid and I would
marry the old man and live with him at
Dun Sithe where Finn would never find us.
I ached with indifference.

The earl saw his chance and
laid hands upon my darling,
counting on the surprise of it to
weigh against his age
but it wasn't enough.
When he called out to me to
help him I took up Diarmuid's own dagger
and stabbed my sweetheart in the thigh.

He stared at the blood and
took himself off, hobbling,
the knife still in the wound.
The earl said he must be dead but I knew
it was never going to be so easy.
I felt his pain. I felt his life persist,
a flame inside my head.

Time passed.
This stranger came, asked could he
roast his salmon at our fire and
could he have water to wash.
He offered me a piece of fish.
When I took it into my mouth
I could smell the honey of our love
on his fingers and knew him for who he was.

He killed the earl with his bare hands.
I hoped he would kill me too but
he stumbled down to the shore
and me after and he was a heron,
alone and grey on the strand.

When he spoke it was only to ask
for a piece of bread.
There was such hunger in him.
Fear seized me and I asked for his knife.
Maybe you should look for it in the
place where you sheathed it last, he said.

I saw that the wound was open,
deep in his thigh, seeping blood,
that the weapon was in the wound still.
My heart aches with shame.
Love is honey and pain and now
I don't know what to do.
Should I free it or let it lie?

* *You will find folk tales of Diarmuid and Grainne throughout Ireland and Scotland. Sometimes it seems as though there is hardly an Iron Age hill fort that is not associated with poor, heroic, relentlessly chaste Diarmuid and beautiful, passionate Grainne. Many years ago, I came across an ancient Scottish version of the tale, collected, as far as I remember, by some diligent folklorist from the School of Scottish Studies, from a Gaelic original, translated into English. Of all the versions, it was this one that seemed the most mysterious to me, so much so, that I used some of the strangely disturbing motifs from it in a novel called Bird of Passage. And I wrote this poem. The images from that original tale still give me a frisson of disquiet.*

## MOZART WAS AN ANGEL

There are wild roses on the road to Chance Inn
curling along the edges of stone walls, and
may, dense, with a heady scent.
Unlucky to pick it.
Unlucky to take it into your home.

I believe that Mozart was an angel
you wrote, but how you
made me cry with your
subtleties, both of you.

Along the road to Chance Inn are
wild roses, fragile, vulnerable.
You put a ring on my finger
but it didn't fit me,
slipped off, much too easily.

If you pick the roses
they will wither in your hands
before you put them in water and
their thorns are very cruel.
Sometimes small rabbits
can't avoid the wheels of
passing cars. Sometimes
there are huddles of
blood and fur in the road.

If we can't forgive who else will?
We have torn each other apart like cobwebs.
I don't love you more than a woman loves her arm.
I manage as a one armed woman
manages how those lost fingers tingle.

There are wild roses curling along the edges of stone walls.
In autumn the hedgerows will be luminous with hips.
In the long grass among campion and vetch
rabbits play.
There are few cars on this
small road that goes only to Chance Inn
and I will drive carefully.

But I think I will never believe in
angels again.

## THE ANGEL IN SAUCHIEHALL STREET

The angel in Sauchiehall Street
floats unnoticed
over the old music emporium,
double flute in hand,
her face intent
her wings a trapeze.

Below, at the seedy side of the street,
the window with its massed bottles
needs cleaning but she's oblivious,
her gaze fixed beyond the river
where her sister's pinned aloft.

A second glance reveals how
she's hemmed in by building.
She would have to fly higher
to find the panorama.
The weight of her own stone
limbs pins her where once
she was a light in the mind.

## CLEANING EVE

They are cleaning Tadolini's Eve
in the Kibble Palace on this hot may morning.
A thousand hands have grimed her skin
cool as a linen sheet.
Two young men dab her leg with cotton wool.
Folk stroke her, one tells me, and indeed
there are black smears along the smooth skin.
She wears a chaste garland of leaves draped
around her hips while outside the blousy tulips riot.
Boys and girls embrace on the grass.
Spring's momentum shifts us all though
I sit alone and rueful in the sun.
The fault lies entirely with me
for desiring my lost gardens.
The lads are texting, all work
forgotten in the urge to make contact
and why not on such a day?
Eve gazes right, distressed.
She's looking for Adam
but the apple was sour, the serpent an excuse.
She knows he won't come.
A toddler stares, flinging his
sun hat in the air and
soon ah soon, she'll be done.

## MOPPING UP

I was telling you about my father
and how the cancer which had run unchallenged
through his body was diagnosed on
the day he died, and how the previous Friday
his boorish doctor had watched me weep,
saying what a difficult man he was
my patient clever kindly dad,
sowing a tiny seed of doubt
which I will never forgive.

I have been thinking about how
in telling you, my friend, I spilled
a cup of water on the cafe table
because years later
my hands still shake when I speak
of this, and how you got up and
fetched paper napkins and mopped
the water, thoughtful and slow
like a man mopping tears,
thoughtful and sad and slow.

## WAITING

Just once, the photograph of my father
at the end of my mother's bed
changes.
Briefly, the filigree and
watered silk frame transforms itself,
into a window through which my dad
watches, serenely, pipe in mouth,
all those years before he gave up smoking.
He's waiting too.

At some point during this year
I find, have found, will find,
his old tobacco jar,
still half full.
It has a rubber seal and when
I open the lid and sniff deeply
the scent brings him back so
vividly that it is a physical
pain in my chest.

For three years I have missed him
most acutely in the morning when I
wake and remember my loss.
Did my mother do the same?
Here in this house where his
walking sticks and his old
cap still inhabit the hallway.
Lifting the lid, sniffing the
fruity scent of his tobacco.
Missing him.

The man in the picture smiles.
Suddenly, I am looking
back at him, the man himself,
through a window onto
somewhere else.

A year has brought us to this point.
A short year, a long year, an
endless year of ups and downs,
of medical neglect,
hopes raised, hopes dashed,
wanting to know,
not wanting to know.
A miserable year, with moments of
hope and despair.

This will be the longest week of my life,
the shortest week of my life,
the saddest and most miraculous.
It comes back to me
in the time between sleeping and waking.
Counsellors call them flashbacks, as though
naming is any solution.
This is a process, fluid and evasive,
rather than a condition,
like the waiting,
which must be endured,
and not so very terrible either.

Once, when the pain of
grief is too acute, I ask for help.
That same night, I dream.
Mum and dad are preparing for an
outing, dressed up to the nines.
She has knitted him a garment of many colours,
the yarns woven into a vivid pattern,
one of her many skills.
But what about me, I say?
You can't come yet, they say.
We do our best, but still it makes you cry
and therefore, us.
Their warmth warms the dreamer too.
Do the dead mourn the living then?

Hospice.
A place of shelter for travellers.
This is the waiting room,
except that my mum,
dearest and only, is nearing the
end of her journey.
Or perhaps not.
Perhaps the journey is much
longer than we realise.
Hospice.
A place of shelter for travellers,
not a terminus at all.

I will remember this place in sunlight.
Red roses clamber up stone walls.
Bees are busy in all the borders.
Mum is too ill for the garden, but
they open the doors and
let the garden come to her.
Inside, there's a table full of flowers
placed where she can see them.

One day, cleaning up mum's house,
I glimpse colour in her greenhouse,
a stray gladiolus, grown enormous in the heat,
tiers of pink flower heads that fluoresce.
I cut it and take it to her.
It dwarfs the vase and the table and
every other blossom in the room:
a flag, a beacon, defiantly alive.

She talks about the future:
having new curtains made,
buying new clothes,
what to get for Christmas.
When I'm better, she says,
pretending for my sake.

This whole year has been as full of
love as an egg is full of meat.
It has been full of anger and despair
but time after time

love has seized me by the
throat and shaken me.
Tough love I didn't know I knew.
Just before the operation
she stood up and hugged me.
The thin sunshine trickled in.
She was thin too, but strong
like light in spring,
stronger than me.
The frailer she became,
the more the light poured through her.

When I was little,
when I was ill, she would
sit by my bed and
sing to me until I slept.
I will not leave her now.
I'm not afraid of dying, she says.
I just want to see your dad again
but I know you don't want me to go.

This is the waiting room.
Train late.
Flight delayed.
The refreshment room.
Strong tea.
Chocolate cake.
A sherry last thing at night.
Tissues for tears.

She has grown so thin that
she is a bird, resting
lightly in the middle of the bed.
She was never a big woman but
she was buxom and pretty.
Nobody could believe that she was seventy.
Do you take your teeth out at night, they asked.
They're a fixture, she said, smiling.

Dad's teeth weren't a fixture.
Three years earlier, when he was dying,
she cleaned his teeth for him and
put them back in for him, and
he smiled and closed his eyes.
Just before he left us
he squeezed my hand.
Now there is almost
nothing left of her and
yet she is still here,
an undeniable presence.

Last week I threw the coins and
read the I Ching.
Life is at an end.
The wild goose seeks for its mate.
She gazes at the little pine wardrobe
on the wall opposite her bed.
She has clothes hanging in there
but she will not wear them again.

She is gathering herself together.
She is not afraid of going, but
she is afraid of being left alone
at the moment of departure
and I think she is afraid for me.

We have waved each other off for years,
small rehearsals for this moment,
waved and turned and blown kisses and waved again.
What a miserable business, this leaving.

My lovely daughter,
are you here? she says.
The last thing she ever says to me.
You'd better have a cup of tea.
Have they given you a cup of tea?
She smiles at me.
I remember one last look,
intense, sad, apologetic.

Still she waits and I wait too.
Her breathing deepens, coarsens, hesitates.
Her pulse flutters.
Then resumes, stronger than ever.
Not yet, not yet.
Can I bear it?
I can.

Days pass and she grows thinner.
Unexpectedly, incongruously,
I think of the death of Falstaff.
*His nose was as sharp as a pen and he babbled of green fields.*
How many years since I was a student,
crying on her shoulder about
small things that loomed large?

My son will not go to school.
Instead he comes and waits a while,
needs my arms around him,
needs the familiar scent of me.
Once, from the garden,
he snatches a glimpse of his nana.
Yes, he says, wisely. She does look different.
Helpers bring trays of tea and home made cakes:
almond slices, sponge cake, chocolate cake.
They laugh among the roses and so do I.

Friends come.
One brings a flask of coffee, hot and strong.
We sit on either side of the bed,
drink it together and laugh,
like people waiting for a train.

I take a walk.
The air smells salty and strange.
I'm a foreigner in this place
so I hurry back. Fearful.
The train might leave without me.

This room is quiet by night.
I lie on my reclining chair,
drift in and out of sleep,
but there are no nightmares.
The only sound is the *crick crack* of the
mattress as the air moves and
eases her fragile bones and the
sinister hiss as the driver administers
another dose of morphine.

There is so little of her left to ease.
Nurses come and turn her tenderly.
They talk to her sweetly,
calling her by her name, and they
treat her kindly and with
dignity, and sometimes
they weep with me.

Grief is celebrated as an aspect of love.
Only physical pain is managed.
There is no question of not waiting.
Waiting is what we do.
In the mornings I take a shower and
resume sitting by the bed.
I'm reading the book my mum
began and will not now finish.
We have both read it many times before.
It made us laugh.
It will make me laugh again.

She's waiting for something, says a nurse.
Or someone.
She looks at the picture of my dad.
A very handsome man, she says.
Tell him he's taking a long time about
doing up that room for her.

We wait because
there is no crime in waiting.
She is no burden.
She is thistledown.
There is no lack of dignity.
There is all the time in the world.

I grow calmer.
What seemed unbearable in prospect is
achieving its own rhythm, the rhythm of waiting.
I no longer lock myself in the lavatory and weep.
I walk in the garden. Settled.
This is by no means the worst time.
Perhaps the worst time is over.

I whisper, you can go now. I'll be alright.
Perhaps she has to know that I mean it,
perhaps she has to be ready,
perhaps it is nothing to do with me at all,
except that I have to be here.
I am part of the process and
this cannot be hurried.

Still she waits,
silky silver hair on the pillow,
skin stretched, translucent, over the
nose that is as sharp as a quill,
over the thin arm resting on the
pretty knitted cover.

Just once, the photograph of
my father, at the end of my
mum's bed, changes.
The filigree and watered silk frame
transforms itself into a window
through which he stares,
pipe in mouth, all those years
before he gave up smoking.
He smiles.
He knows.

On the seventh day,
in the afternoon,
her breathing changes again
and shudders and slows and stops.
Hands hold me, her, me.
Blessings are given and received.
There is no pain or panic.
This is exactly the right time.
Everything is happening just as it should.
The expression that crosses her
face is one of mild surprise, a
raising of the eyebrows.

Not pain, just surprise.
There you are, Julian, she would say.
And then she is gone, as surely as a setting sun.

I take off her watch, the
watch my dad gave her, and
slip it onto my wrist.
I take off my watch, the watch my dad gave me, and
slip it onto her wrist and leave it there.
It just seems the thing to do.

Afterwards the nurses
pack up her clothes,
her slippers, her pretty nighties,
neatly laundered, the tablet of soap
I bought for her on the fancy goods stall at the
church garden party, a couple of weeks ago.
We drive home in sunshine.
I sleep and sleep and sleep.

In the morning
I find that the ache of dad without mum has gone.
Also the unbearable burden of her grief.
I am left only with my own and
that is easier to bear.

When I open the door of their house the
scent of home comes rushing out to meet me.
The place is warm but they are not here.
They have always been adventurous,
embracing new experiences with enthusiasm.
Hopeful travellers.

They have left a message.
The last time we went out together,
Mum bought hibiscus plants for us
but hers lay quiescent for weeks.
On the windowsill I find it in bloom again.
Two glowing trumpets stand side by side,
staring up and out towards the distant hills.
Do the dead mourn? Was dad waiting too?
Were all of us waiting for precisely the right time?

## SCHEHERAZADE

Maybe this time she said,
we should tell each other stories.
At least we can begin by
bridging the years
spinning words
weaving a net
strong enough to catch us
when we fall.

Fall he said.
From grace she said.
Love goes without saying.

Sometimes said the king
it speaks all too plainly
but goes anyway.

You always had a
way with words she said.

We could try said the king
but haven't we done this before?
And nobody lived
happily ever after.

Ah but that was once upon a time
when we were young and
distracted by mutual desire and
neither of us would have been
happy with narrative then.

Are you content with words now he said
Is this any better?
I worry about you.
He had always been protective for all
she had feared he might
chop off her head.

She remembered how weary they had been
at the end and how at last she had
left an unfinished story
hoping perhaps to provoke
some response and how
he had done nothing,
no retribution,
no axes had fallen,
only a terrible silence.

It was for your own good
he said and besides there were
mitigating circumstances.
I seem to have been an
an unreliable narrator
and I'm sorry she said.
Me too he said. Oh me too.

She thought about the five hundred and one
untold tales which had been
swallowed by silence.
She thought of their shared pleasure in words.
They had barely scratched the surface.

If words are all we have he said
then for pity's sake
tell me another story.

## NEVER KNIT A SWEATER FOR A MAN

Twenty years later, clearing out a cupboard,
she comes across a plastic bag containing
the remains of a sweater she had been knitting,
Fair-Isle, tricky, half a dozen yarns carried forward
and woven into a complex textile which was
she remembers - she has never done it since -
a task requiring the utmost concentration.

She pulls it out, unfolding a back,
a single spiralled sleeve, an unfinished front
still on the needles and barely past the rib
with holes here and there where moths
have eaten their way in, feasting on her work
and at the bottom of the bag a few
skeins of wool, their colours dulled
and inexplicably tangled by time.

When did she lose the thread,
the will to see it through to the bitter end?
Was it after she and its intended recipient had
unravelled or was it even earlier?
Was it, she now sees, always beyond her skills,
a garment too difficult to be contrived by human hand
let alone worn?

She peers into the bag wondering what if anything
can be salvaged but the dust lodged
deep in the fibres brings a tear to her eyes
and makes her sneeze.
Bless you she says and throws it in the bin.

## UNDERSTANDING SALOME

And after all, she loved to dance,
not just for her stepfather but for herself.
No man ever seems to note how
women dance only for themselves.

Can't you just hear beardie John,
up to his armpits in water, rabbiting on,
telling anyone who would listen
they were doomed but especially
those inconveniently bleeding females?

So perhaps she was sick of his
lack of compassion.
All that water, a whole river,
could not wash away
his contempt for those
womanly things she cherished.

Maybe she foresaw as much as he.
Maybe it was an attempt to save
her sisters for all time from
self righteous censure.

Or maybe it was simply a joke.
Poor poor Salome,
forgetting that men
are persistently literal.
Feeling ill? See a doctor then!

I'll tell you what I want.
I'll tell you what would make me happy.
That bastard's bloody head upon a platter.

## DADDY MY

Dad, dead these fourteen years,
came to the door in a dream last night.
He still does this, a little less
often perhaps, but always
with a wee ache of normality.

I rushed through the room to
take his hand which
seemed oddly cool and small.
In life his hands were warm and
chipped and tinted with paint.
He was a dad who fixed things

Waking I remember how
the Railway Children makes me cry
with my incurable need to be Bobbie
in that daddy my daddy moment
meeting my own perfect train.

## SAILING AWAY *(for alan)*

We move out of the harbour.
You have the advantage of me.
You know each cloud,
its name and what it brings.
I struggle with unfamiliarity.

The land recedes, relinquishes us
and the bright sails sting our eyes.
I can hardly see you in all this light
but stretch out cold fingers
to touch your face.

We move far out,
much further than I planned.
But still, she holds us
safe in warmth inside.
We two in our same boat.

## APART

We sit around a few heaped coals of fire.
Outside the summer rain drenches
leaves, grass, brown lilac.
The spring is done and summer hesitates
between.

They are talking among themselves
of how to live and how to work and
how they do. Nice people all, their
words vibrate through the quiet room.
Everything matters.

On the hearthrug, the cat
opens one yellow eye and yawns and
stretches a skittish armoured paw.
She does not care, she does not give a
damn. Defends herself, contained.

And I? I am here between the two.
My head is full of sweet summer rain
and I am thinking of you.
I am thinking of you.

## POWERCUT

Last night we had a powercut.
Over the village the stars
resumed their proper places.
Our guests left by the light of
candles already burning.

We cleared dishes, patiently
restored what order we could.
Shadows obscured corners.
Small flames danced to their
reflections or flickered over
wood brought suddenly to life.

In the sitting room the
fire pulsed. I paused
listening to the near silence.
No television blared,
no glib radio, no music
spilled from space to space.

But the wind droned
faintly in the chimney as
the house hunkered down,
curled its tail, purring,
and I knew with more than
certainty that there are those
here who still prefer it this way.

## HARVEST

In the heat of a September afternoon,
I'm late as usual, foraging among hedgerow nettles,
hawthorn and fading honeysuckle for a few brambles.
People have been here before me.
I see the marks of their feet,
pressing pathways in the damp grass.
I'm distracted by sloes and rosehips.
Everything nips, bites, pinches and stings but
I'm peaceful, the pain a necessary distraction.
I hear tractors, steaming ahead in this fine spell,
and the echo and dunt of a hammer at Windyhill
where someone is mending something.
A surprised horse lifts its head and blows a greeting.
Desperate wasps harass.
Birds panic at my footfall.
Tomorrow I'll mix these few fruits with
apples from our Golden Noble tree,
to bake a pie in the sky blue dish Keith made.
Tomorrow I'll prick these glossy fruits
till my hands are black and
make gin for winter.
But today, a stranger pauses, her car full of sleeping
children.
Still unfamiliar with these ways, are they sloes,
are those blackthorns, she asks, bewildered.
I think of ruby liquid warming winter nights.
I tell her my harvest.
I pass it on.

## THE SCENT OF BLUE

A concert in Edinburgh, years ago.
She manages to find a single seat,
sees a famous conductor,
silver haired, sharp featured, like some
bird of prey, but smaller than you would
expect in evening dress.
On his arm, a thin woman,
taller than he is, strides with
striking face and hair, a nimbus of
grey blonde curls around her head.
Not a young woman but a
diva surely, inhabiting her clothes,
inhabiting her skin with such confidence.
She wants to be like that some day,
longs for self possession
and she remembers the scent of her,
musky, mysterious, a heavy, night time
scent, like flowers after dark.
The scent of passion.
The scent of money.
The scent of blue.

She searches for the scent for years.
Her mother wore Tweed.
Now she wishes she could
open a wardrobe door, and
smell her mother's oakmoss scent,
almost as much as she
wishes she could tell her mother so.

As a girl, she wears Bluebell,
fresh and full of hope, or
Diorissimo, like the lilac she once
carried through the streets,
on her way from meeting a man
she desired and admired, thinking
Girl with Lilac, still so young,
self conscious, not possessed.

Later, she tries l'Air du Temps and
Je Reviens and Fleurs de Rocaille
but they are none of them the scent of blue.
She wears Chanel, briefly, with dreams of Marilyn,
loves to watch her, loves to hear her voice,
soothing as chocolate, but
Five is not her scent,
never suits her, never will.

She discovers Mitsouko.
Some tester in some chemist's shop.
An old, old fashioned scent,
syncopated, unexpected, not to every taste.
Whenever she wears it,
women ask her what it is.
How strange the way scent lingers in the mind.
How strange the way scent
changes on warm skin.
On her it ripens into something peachy,
mossy, rich and rare.
But it is not the scent of blue.

She loses her heart.
It is an affair of telephone lines
more profound, more sweet and
bitter than Mitsouko,
a doomed song in the dark,
and the colour of that time is blue.

Afterwards, she searches through
Bellodgia, L'Aimant,
Emeraude, l'Interdit,
until drawn by nostalgia
she finds Joy.
Finds roses and jasmine,
a summer garden in one small bottle.
She marries in Joy,
but she wears Mitsouko
and she forgets the scent of blue.

Older, she discovers Calandre and then Arpège,
not just rose and jasmine but
bergamot, orange blossom, peach, vanilla, ylang ylang,
one essence piled on another like the notes on the piano
she used to, sometimes still does, play.
Oh this is not a scent for the very young.
It is too dark for that
a memory of something lost,
an unfinished story.
This scent has a past.

She sees him across a room.
Another woman ushers him,
this way and that, makes introductions,
a little charmed the way women
always did flutter around this man.
It used to make her smile, the way
women flocked around this
wolf who walked alone, who
belonged to nobody but himself.

She is wearing Arpège.
Not a scent for the very young,
vertiginous as the layers of time between.
With age comes wisdom,
but as when mud is
stirred at the bottom of a pool,
memories bubble to the surface.
Not wisely but too well they loved.
Now, they wave across the years.
They speak, in measured tones,
they speak in careful words, that
every now and then
recall the scent of

No.
It will not do.
Only in dreams
can one innocently recapture that
first fine careless

So much more is forgotten
than is ever remembered
and the clock says
let it be let it be
and they do.

1911
One summer evening
a young man observes the way twilight closes the
flowers,
whose scent lingers on the last heat of the day,
the way the light goes out of the sky,
painting it dark blue, how
soon the war will tear this place apart.
How soon all things resort to sadness.

In a new century,
She finds among jasmine and rose,
vanilla and violet,
a dark twist of anise, like the
twist of a knife.
First last always.
The scent of the diva.
The scent of passion.
Fine beyond imagining,
she sees it is essentially
sad, sad, sad, a
sad scent.
L'Heure Bleue.
All things come to sadness in the end.
The beautiful bitter foolish scent of blue.

## ON THE BEACH AT CULZEAN

### WINTER

The black dog rushes ahead. She is more than ten years dead, but here she is, sniffing along the shoreline, her curly cockade of a tail held high. My son, in red wellies and padded jacket, is walking along the beach, squatting to examine a handful of minute golden shells, prising them up with his starfish fingers, toddler's treasure.

The shore is a string of pebbly and sandy curves. Arran comes and goes: a grey space, a smudge, a real place, etched against the skyline, Goat Fell cloaked in snow. The sea is audible on all but the stillest of days but in winter it is a muted roar. Closer, you can distinguish the inward rush and outward tug of pebbles beneath the waves. Agates have tumbled in, eggs that shatter against the rocks to reveal a smooth world within a world, a blue and white landscape, sea and sky preserved in stone.

The effect of the cliffs, the woods, is to shield the beaches from change, cutting them off from the land. Up there are narrow paths, leading mysteriously out of sight. Some of them thread through frosted plants and naked trees to the sea. Some of them end in nothing, nowhere, oblivion. Take care.

One winter, a canon blew down from the castle and landed on the beach. On Boxing Day, we took coffee and Christmas cake and climbed down to the empty bay, to sit on the elephantine rocks and gaze at the sea. Grey on grey. We found it half submerged in a pool of water, an intruder in this wholly wild world.

## SPRING

My son has shed his wellies and hooded coat, casting his clouts before may is out. He slides and slithers, exclaiming over each find: fishing net, feathers, sea glass, his voice bouncing off rocks. What creature made these holes? What's gribble worm? What? Why? How?

In the woods, snowdrops have given place to windflowers, then daffodils, ramsons, bluebells. On the fringes of the park, there are swathes of whin that smell of coconut and dazzle the eyes. During hard times farmers pulped this spiny crop and fed it to their cattle. The whin mill was an upended grindstone, trundled along a channel, hauled by a carthorse. You can see ghostly rings in the grass, to this day. And whin is still hard to handle. Stumble, put out a hand to save yourself and there will be tears.

Down here, the shore is edged by volcanic rocks, stretched and folded back on themselves, wrinkled, with seams of white quartz. There are caves too with ancient fortifications built across, as though the earlier castle had grown upwards, a living thing, rooted in the rocks beneath. Archaeologists have found human bones here. People were born in these caves, spent their lives, died and were buried among the giant spiders that also call this labyrinth home.

On the beach, the storms have left a litter of driftwood behind, sculptures on smooth sand. Out there the air is a mixture of salt and sweet. Ailsa Craig is a sugared cake.

Picnic time. From above, you can see reefs at low tide, with cormorants and shags perched on the teeth of them. They teem with life, these pavements of rock, and the pools between: anemones, barnacles, little fishes, translucent shrimps, sea slugs. Children are exploring the reefs, teasing the anemones, briefly imprisoning creatures in jars and boxes. Look and let go, look and let go, calls the teacher.

We trek down to the beach, staggering beneath our trappings. We make a boat out of sand. My son motors to Arran and back within the hour and the sand holds up pretty well. He and his father and his grandfather commence engineering operations. My mother and I are admiring spectators. They dam the burn that trickles down from the hill, dig a new channel, build a castle, divert the channel so that it forms a moat. The whole edifice is decorated with shells and white quartz pebbles.

There are swallows diving above, oystercatchers patrolling the shoreline, wagtails darting here and there. I tuck my skirt into my knickers and wade through soft salt water, feeling shells between my toes, then look back and see the men in my life, grown small against the rocks, utterly absorbed in the moment and each other.

The dog follows me, splashing and cavorting. She has found a length of mooring rope, thick and prickly, but it is pinned into the shallows by a stone, and she is pulling and tugging, snuffling and sneezing as the salt water goes up her nose. Up there, behind the theatrical arc of the beach, people are walking among the scenery, wearing unsuitable shoes. You can see the odd flash of colour from a jacket or dress. There are precarious girls in high heeled sandals, tight skirts pinning their knees together. The air smells of roses.

My son is growing fast. He wears a burgundy waterproof against the rain and a daft tweed hat that suits him, although he will only wear it here, where his friends won't see. He has given up holding hands. But he still has apples in his cheeks, and a face like a flower, open and trusting. My heart aches for him, for all those leaps of faith which he must soon make. For the tripping and falling. For the spiny shrubs. For the picking himself up and walking on. For the narrowing of possibilities. For the disappointments and the friendships and the loves that are not me. How could it be otherwise?

Geese skein across the sky. The swallows have already gone. We stumble down the path to the sea past the boathouse with its tarry roof. The old dog with her white muzzle trots ahead of us. She comes and goes, a memory in both our heads.

Down here on Culzean beach, the familiarity of these stones, these shells, these grains of sand is comforting, our apprehensions soothed by the relentless thrust and pull of the sea. There is only now.

Behind the cliffs behind the woods there has been a change of scene. The heather is in bloom. The hill is a paisley shawl.

## ACKNOWLEDGEMENTS

Among various collections, and magazines, many of which no longer exist, these poems have been published in:

**White Boats**, an anthology with Andrew Greig, Garret Arts 1973

**Workshop New Poetry** Number 23: Edited by Norman Hidden, 1974

**Akros**: Edited by Duncan Glen 1975

**Scottish Love Poems**, a personal anthology by Antonia Fraser, Canongate 1975

**Pembroke Magazine** Number 7: Edited by Trevor Royle, 1976

**A Book of Men and Other Poems** by Catherine Czerkawska, Akros Publications, 1976

**Scottish Poetry Nine**: Edited by Maurice Lindsay, Alexander Scott and Roderick Watson, 1976

**AMF** Dundee 1977

**Words 5**: Edited by Carl MacDougall 1978

**Lines Review** Number 68: Edited by William Montgomerie 1979

**Aquarius** Number 11: Edited by Eddie Linden, 1979

**Lines Review** Number 73: Edited by William Montgomerie 1980

**Identities**: Edited by Geddes Thomson, 1981

**Noise and Smoky Breath**: Edited by Hamish Whyte 1983

**The Scent of Blue**, poems by Catherine Czerkawska 2007
**The Brownsbank Broadsheet** Number 1: Edited by Carl MacDougall, 2009
**Scottish Cats**, an anthology: edited by Hamish Whyte 2013
**I'm Coming With You**, Scottish PEN, 2017

There were a great many poets, writers and academics who encouraged me when I was writing poetry, but among those who are no longer with us, a special mention must go to my English tutor, Ronnie Jack, to Duncan Glen of Akros, to George Mackay Brown, who corresponded with me, to Ian Hamilton Finlay, whose own work was inspirational, to Robert Garioch, who was very kind to a young writer finding her feet, and finally to my funny, iconoclastic friend, Paul Edwards, who was never less than supportive but who taught me to keep both feet firmly on the ground.

## ABOUT THE AUTHOR

Catherine Czerkawska is an extensively published writer of fiction (novels and short stories) non-fiction, poetry and award-winning plays for theatre, BBC radio and television. Born in Yorkshire, of Polish and Irish parentage, she has spent most of her life in Scotland, with time also spent working in Finland, Poland and the Canaries.

Her many novels include *The Physic Garden*, set in early nineteenth-century Glasgow, *The Curiosity Cabinet*, *The Posy Ring* and *The Jewel*, a meticulously researched novel about the life and times of Robert Burns's wife, Jean Armour. *Bird of Passage* and *The Amber Heart* are family sagas of cruelty, loss and enduring love. *A Proper Person to be Detained* and *The Last Lancer* are poignant true histories that take us from 19th century Ireland and WW2 Poland to the industrial heartlands of England and Scotland.

Her stage plays include two full length plays commissioned by Edinburgh's Traverse Theatre: *Wormwood*, a play about the Chernobyl disaster, staged in 1997, and Quartz. She has written plays for Glasgow's Oran Mor, as well as various community theatre projects, television drama and more than 100 hours of drama for BBC R4.

Her other interests include antique textiles, vintage perfumes, local and social history. She has served on the committee of the Society of Authors in Scotland and spent four years as Royal Literary Fund Writing Fellow at the University of the West of Scotland.

www.catherineczerkawska.co.uk